STEAM MOTIVE POWER CENTRES:

No.2: CREWE

Including: The Locomotive Works, Engine S

BOOK LAW PUBLICATIONS

INTRODUCTION

The work of amateur photographer Don Beecroft is fairly well-known in the contemporary railway magazines catering for the steam enthusiast of yesteryear. However, this album is one of a number being produced to show off his work exclusively. Building on images from the mid-1950's to the end of steam on BR, from Penzance to Thurso, we have put together an interesting series covering specific locations or regions.

This particular album gives us an insight of one specific location dear to many of us, at least in the period under review - the late 1950's early 60's. The place of course is Crewe, its engine sheds, station and the gigantic locomotive works. Recorded over numerous weekend visits, the images recorded on film give us a great insight to the working railway of that period. The filth, grime, neglect and overall greyness of those times is balanced with pictures of gleaming newness, obvious pride in some jobs and hopelessness in others. What stands out, perhaps, is the sheer scale of British Railways as an organisation able to repair, build and then get rid of its own motive power fleet on a basis of renew when necessary.

On a more personal note, notice from the Crewe Works images especially, that Don managed to record the steam locomotives without introducing any of their diesel counterparts into the background. The new motive power was all over the place at the time but none of them got a peep into the frame.

(*previous page*) **Crewe station, north end, July 1957. 'Royal Scot' No.46162 waits for the road to Crewe North shed for turning, coaling, watering, fire and smokebox cleaning before working back home to Carlisle.** *BLP - DB3435.*

Printed and bound by The Amadeus Press, Cleckheaton, West Yorkshire.
First published in the United Kingdom by Book Law Publications, 382 Carlton Hill, Nottingham, NG4 1JA

June 1958, Crewe North engine shed. Local boy - 71000 DUKE OF GLOUCESTER stands on No.4 road of the so-called 'Middle' shed. The engine is fully coaled and about ready to head the Down *MID-DAY SCOT* northwards to Glasgow on its afternoon journey through northern England. Already some four years old, the unique BR Standard 8P Pacific was virtually half way through its operational life by this time. Through some oversight during its design and construction, which have been 'rectified' in its second life as a preserved engine, No.71000 did not live up to expectations and was not one of the favourite engines amongst the 5A fleet. However, it was not a total damp squid and in the right enthusiastic and knowledgeable hands it could still put in some good performances on the WCML albeit at the cost of a high coal consumption. 'The Duke' was a regular on *THE MID-DAY SCOT* virtually up to the time of its premature retirement in 1962. Much has been written about its lacklustre showing during BR days but it was a victim of the 'Modernisation Plan' when nearly all steam locomotive testing and evaluation was curtailed. Perhaps, given a few more years, or even months, to find and eliminate the minor problems which irritated so many locomotive engineers and footplate crews, BR might have enlarged the class from this solitary example. The writer still finds it amazing that a bunch of dedicated enthusiasts ended up being the ones who put right what so many professionals could not. *BLP - DB760.*

3

In a near perfect photographic pose with its connecting rods in the lowest position, resident 'Coronation' No.46252 CITY OF LEICESTER rests inside the semi-roundhouse in March 1960. This new engine shed had been completed during the previous October and was about a third of the size originally planned for the site. In fact, two interconnecting roundhouses had been envisaged during the early planning stages for the total reconstruction of Crewe North motive power depot and this section would have been but a segment of the No.2 shed. Indeed, had the scheme been carried through the depot would have become the ultimate in steam locomotive sheds with sixty-four stabling roads radiating from two 70ft articulated turntables. However, in the end this was all that was provided for locomotive accommodation. The No.2 size coaling plant and twin ash disposal plants, which were another major component of the modernisation at 5A, were built and became operational by 1951. There was to be another set of identical devices on the eastern side of the yard, serving the proposed No.1 roundhouse. No doubt the early completion of this first group of concrete edifices brought about a greater efficiency in the servicing and disposal of Crewe North's prestige stud. But, modern undercover stabling eventually came down to just this 12-road building. The giant 12-road 'Middle' shed, complete with drop pit, shear legs and 800 yards of track under its roof, sufficed for repair, maintenance and other purposes. One of the green liveried members of its class, No.46252 did not end its days working from Crewe North, instead, three months after this view was captured, it transferred to Carlisle Upperby shed then, just nine months before withdrawal, it moved south to Camden for a last fling which included a long period of storage. Withdrawn on the first day of June 1963, it returned to Crewe in September for scrapping at the Works. *BLP - DB3131.*

Another 5A resident inside the semi roundhouse that day in March 1960, was 'Jubilee' No.45634 TRINIDAD. Looking far from resplendent but nevertheless in steam, the 4-6-0 had about the same length of operational life left as the Pacific. By now TRINIDAD was chasing any work that was entrusted to it and in November 1960, to help out with the pre-Christmas traffic, it moved to Willesden shed but returned north to Crewe in January. This time though it was allocated to Crewe South shed where fitted freights, parcel trains, secondary passenger trains and unfitted goods were more or less the daily grind. In May 1963, with a major repair pending but never received, No.45634 was withdrawn and put into storage to await the call from its birthplace. It was cut up at the Works in August 1963, a year short of a thirty year life. *BLP - DB3134.*

The two open-air stabling roads of the partially completed roundhouses add a bit more space to the depot's 'parking' facilities in March 1960. The wall of the roundhouse is of course a temporary screen, easily removeable once the extension was built. In the event, the completion of the roundhouse did not take place, money ran out, ideas and plans were changed, steam was finished. In the meantime the residents got on with it. 'Brit' No.70017 ARROW has some years left in front of it yet. Resident 'Scot' No.46155 THE LANCER does not have a lot of time left in comparison but note the yellow prohibition stripe on the cabside. This application must have been one of the earliest because the overhead wires were nowhere near completion south of Crewe and would not be for some time. *BLP - DB3127.*

Visiting 'Jubilee' No.45742 CONNAUGHT had spent a couple of stints allocated to Crewe North during its lifetime but in March 1960 it was part of the Upperby allocation. It was to end its days in May 1965 working from Carlisle but at Kingmoor shed where it moved to in July 1962 along with ten other Upperby based 'Jubilee's' Nos.45588, 45678, 45680, 45681, 45688, 45703, 45731, 45734, 45738 and 45741. Its late withdrawal saw it purchased by a private scrap metal contractor and in August 1965 it was towed to Motherwell for scrapping. Behind the engine is an unidentified BR Standard Class 5, looking in virtually the same unkempt condition as the 'namer'. Above the 'Standard' looms the dilapidated roof of the so-called 'Abyssinia' shed, another 12-road structure which, by March 1960, had been cut back somewhat from its original length to make room for the depot alterations which were never fulfilled. Note the paved area which up to 1953 had been roofed in. Locomotives were still using the shed for stabling but the building was virtually ready for falling down. *BLP - DB3136.*

7

Stabled alongside the east wall of the new 'roundhouse', 'Royal Scot' No.46159 THE ROYAL AIR FORCE still carries the old BR emblem on its tender in March 1960. This Derby built engine was one of the early recipients of the 2A taper boiler, being one of eleven 'Scots' converted in 1945. Up to that conversion the engine had been variously allocated to seven different sheds: Camden, Crewe North, Holyhead, Longsight, Preston, Rugby and Upperby, although not in that order. When BR came into being it had settled down somewhat being 'shared' by two depots, Camden and Crewe North. Throughout the 1950's it virtually ping-ponged between these two sheds annually although when this scene was recorded it was a firm resident of 5A but not for much longer as London beckoned once more. This time, however, it was Camden's down market but somewhat larger relation Willesden which took in the 4-6-0 in January 1961. By the summer of the following year No.46159 was back at Crewe, slightly rundown and in need of overhaul, it was taken into the Works during September but was left to languish throughout the bitter winter. By the end of February 1963 it was a pile of scrap. *BLP - DB3135.*

It wasn't all Brunswick green, Crimson Lake and 'namers' at Crewe North. Some of the railway systems' more menial engines could be seen during visits to the place. In March 1960 motor fitted Ivatt Class 2 tank No.41220 and Fowler Cl.4 No.42362 of Stoke, share a stabling road outside the 'Middle' shed in the afternoon sunshine. The 2-6-2t was a resident of 5A, had been since May 1958 when it came looking for push-pull work. Latterly it had been around seeking such employment at Bangor, Bushbury, Wellingborough, Watford and now Crewe. Its options were diminishing daily as branch lines and uneconomical services were abandoned. The Crewe to Northwich via Sandbach passenger services were its prime purposes for being at 5A. It left Crewe North in July 1963 for Llandudno Junction shed but after a couple of years there it moved on to Edgeley shed having give up the push-pull business. Withdrawn in November 1966, the handy little Class 2 tank rotted at Stockport for more than six months before being purchased for scrap by Cashmore's at Great Bridge, the same scrapyard where the older Fowler tank had ended up some four years before. Note the catenary of the 25kV electrification spanning the main line at the north end of the station over to the left. *BLP - DB3126.*

In the precarious world of BR steam during its last decade of existence, a problem such as that being suffered in March 1960 by Nuneaton based 7F 0-8-0 No.49440 could be fatal. Obviously something has happened to either the axleboxes or the inside valve gear but it was not deemed serious enough to have the former LNWR Class G2 towed across to the nearby works for attention in the shops or, more likely, scrapping. The other G2 behind is No.49377 from Edge Hill. Whatever circumstance had brought two of these ancient eight-coupled goods engines on to Crewe North is not known but it was unusual at that period to have a pair of these engines at 5A when normally their quarters at Crewe would have been the South depot. No.49440 did eventually get a one-way tow into the Works but it was exactly two years after this event, in March 1962 when it was condemned and broken up, aged thirty-nine years and seven months. The even older No.49377 lasted a little bit longer. Withdrawn in October 1962, it was taken into Crewe works for scrapping in April 1963 - aged sixty years and five months. *BLP - DB3132.*

Llandudno Junction shed had been home to a number of these Caprotti equipped Class 5's from their introduction in 1948. Indeed of the five initially allocated to that depot in June/July 1948 - 44738 to 44742 - only one, No.44740, spent the whole of its operational life at 'the Junction'. Others came and went but this engine managed to evade the transfer list for fifteen years. Crewe North shed played host to these 6G engines on a daily basis when they worked in on some passenger turn or other from the North Wales coast. As for the other 'normal' types of Class 5, Crewe North had dozens of them on its books; only places such as Perth and perhaps Kingmoor had a larger allocation. In this March 1960 picture the 4-6-0 is ready to work home and is standing on the preparation pits which by then were being used as a place to stable 'foreign' engines after they had been serviced. On entering Crewe Works for repair in March 1963, No.44740 was condemned and scrapped shortly afterwards. Behind the Caprotti is 5A resident Stanier Mogul No.42966. *BLP - DB3129.*

11

Another class with a long association to Crewe North engine shed was the Stanier version of the Horwich 'Crab'. No.42966 is ready, it seems, for a northbound working in this March 1960 view on the shed yard. Note the setting of the coal in the Fowler tender has been placed to maximise the load. Perhaps wherever the engine was headed did not have such as good a quality of coal as 5A and therefore the crew would if possible, abstain from topping up the tender with indifferent fuel. Besides No.42966, Crewe north had five other Stanier moguls at this time, Crewe South shed had ten of them on the books. In the background is 'Coronation' No.46235 CITY OF BIRMINGHAM yet another of the green Pacifics. *BLP - DB3130.*

THE DUMPS

About two miles north of Norton Bridge station, in sidings situated on both sides of the West Coast main line, there suddenly appeared in 1959 a load of dumped steam locomotives. Now about this time 'dumps' containing dozens of redundant and withdrawn steam locomotives began to spring up all over the BR system. Some were large in extent, some were small. Heapey Bridge in Lancashire comes to mind, so does the Over & Wharton branch line in Cheshire (*see* lpage 15), Bo'ness in Scotland, and lots of other locations became a sign of the times. It wasn't just engine sheds where withdrawn engines could be seen, now they began to materialise out in the country. The site near Norton Bridge was called Badnall Wharf and in the scale of size could have been regarded as small to medium. On the Up side in April 1959 were just four locomotives, all of pre-Group origin. They were Nos.50777, 50855, 51453, 58066 - three ex Lanky's and a Midland 0-4-4T. In this view we can see sections of two of them and the Middy tank. They are, left to right: 51453, 58066 and 50777. No.50855 was just out of picture to the south of 50777. All the engines were intact except for their former shedplates. Their destination was Crewe Works, for scrapping, but that establishment was not quite ready for this steady trickle of scrap metal yet and it would be August 1959 before the new Scrap Shop was ready to recommence cutting up and some of the Badnall Wharf's temporary residents made their final journey north. *BLP - DB1409.*

Across the main line in the Down side siding in April 1959, amongst a load of Conflats bearing meat containers, the crowd was much bigger and was getting bigger by the week. Here, in numerical order were: 41078, 41156, 41724, 41936, 43419, 43631, 50646, 50725, 50757, 50818, 50831, 50865, 51424, 52399, 52517, 58196. Again the mixture is L&Y and MR. Getting reasonable pictures amongst all the wagons and shrubbery was not too easy and when ex Lanky 2-4-2T No.50831 was snapped, its front end was partly obscured by the bunker of 50757. Later in the year others began to appear and amongst those were the first of the LMS Standard classes to be affected. We knew then that as far as steam traction went the rot had set in. However, the speed at which the condemnations took place astonished most of us. It became a matter of urgency to get out and photograph as much as possible, especially steam locomotives lying dead in sidings. Later arrivals at Badnall Wharf included: 40021, 40052, 41158, 41797, 43192, 43219, 43248, 43315, 43318, 43335, 43339, 43379, 43388, 43433, 43558, 43619, 43623, 43630, 43674, 43728, 47191, 47247, 58171, 58198. By the middle of 1961 the sidings had stored their last steam locomotives. Crewe Works was scrapping condemned locomotives as fast as they arrived from the sheds but by then other larger operators had been invited to join the quest to exterminate BR steam and a number of the occupants of these sidings went to the private scrapyards. *BLP - DB1410.*

Somewhat nearer to Crewe, at Winsford, a short branch line diverged off the Down side of the West Coast Main Line about eight miles north of Crewe. The former LNWR line was called the Over & Wharton branch and had closed in 1947, at least to passenger traffic. If, prior to 1959, it was virtually unknown amongst railway enthusiasts, then by the summer of that year it was certainly infamous and was visited by literally thousands who could make it there. Here, in the midst of the quiet Cheshire countryside in early 1959, British Railways started to store dozens of redundant steam locomotives which were awaiting entry to Crewe Works for scrapping. By May 1959 there were more than thirty engines stored on the old branch. The engines could be grouped into two different lots, LNW in origin and LMS with heavy Midland influence. This is G2a No.48945, one of a dozen ex LNW 0-8-0s resident at that time. Withdrawn during the previous month from Shrewsbury shed, the fifty-six year old never made it into Crewe and was instead sold for scrap to a private contractor in South Wales. None of the other 0-8-0s in the following list were cut up at Crewe either, all of them ending up being purchased by two contractors. During Don Beecroft's visit the following thirty-three engines were languishing on the branch: 41928, 41939, 41941, 41945, 41946, 41948, 41950, 41977, 41978, 41982, 41983, 41984, 41985, 41986, 41987, 41990, 41991, 41992, 41993, 48905, 48945, 49010, 49109, 49113, 49117, 49157, 49180, 49226, 49228, 49308, 49330, 49368, 49409. By February 1960 the branch once again returned to its quiet derelict state, the year long occupancy by the unwanted, dead steam locomotives was over; they had all be towed away to various destinations for scrap. *BLP - DB1426.*

Ex-works G2a No.49134 rests on Crewe South shed in March 1960, ready for another two years hard labour prior to withdrawal. A Nuneaton engine and nearly fifty years old at the time of this photograph, the 0-8-0 managed to partake in two more shed transfers - Preston and Patricroft - before entering Crewe Works for the last time. Behind is one of South shed's Stanier moguls whilst at the other end of the shed is an English Electric Type 4 diesel. Notice the state of the shed roof, with cladding composed of either corrugated asbestos or that old wartime favourite corrugated iron. Whatever it was made of was still being held up by the original northlight trussing from when the shed was built in 1897. All that was changing and in one of the last engine shed repairs carried out by BR, South shed got a new roof over eight of its roads during the next few months. The remaining four roads were left open to the elements. *BLP - DB2987.*

Crewe South shed was the main reception point for engines leaving the Locomotive Works after overhaul and those engines attending Works, be it for overhaul or breaking up. Two engines ready for overhaul in March 1960 were 'Jubilee' No.45560 PRINCE EDWARD ISLAND and an unidentified Stanier 8F. The 'Jubilee' was at that time allocated to Edge Hill shed and appears to be dire need of a clean never mind an overhaul. However, both will be administered whilst it is in the shops and to give it a good start for the final three years of active life it will also receive a fresh coat or two of paint. In June 1961 in its final move over a twenty-nine year career No.45560 would transfer to Crewe North shed. Built by the North British Locomotive Co. in 1934, the engine was not named until 1936 by which time most of the class had been given names to celebrate locations within the British Empire, famous admirals, and warships - such were the heady days of the 1930's. In January 1964 this particular 'Jubilee' entered Crewe Works for the last time and was cut up. Luckily its nameplates survived to remind us of our historical past. *BLP - DB2989.*

Further along the Works line that day in March 1960 was this neglected Class G2a 0-8-0 No.49116. Withdrawn during the previous November at Edge Hill shed, the fifty year old veteran was now just a few weeks away from being scrapped at its birthplace. *BLP - DB2990.*

Since the earliest days of diesel motive power on the LMS Crewe South shed had housed a contingent of shunting locomotives to work the Basford Hall yard and its surrounding sidings. In March 1960 one of the older inhabitants of this growing fleet at 5B was No.12010 a diesel-electric version which had a jackshaft drive. Built at Derby in December 1939, its LMS number had been 7087 but BR renumbered it in May 1948. Of the initial forty strong class, all built between 1939 and 1942, ten were allocated to Crewe South from new, others went to Kingmoor, Toton and Willesden, however, ten of the locomotives built in 1941 went directly to the War Department and never returned to the LMS with most leaving the country for the Middle East theatre. Others, from the 1942 batch, were employed for a short period by the WD but were returned to the LMS that same year. No.12010 ended its days at Speke Junction engine shed being withdrawn from there in September 1967 and later sold for scrap. Note the new catenary in the background and, nearer the camera, the fuelling point and new engine pit. Crewe South had been home for many diesel locomotives since 1936 and most gravitated around the north end of the shed where the relevant facilities were installed. *BLP - DB2988.*

Sister engine to No.12010, 12009 looked to be in far better shape in March 1960, after what appears to have been a visit to Derby for overhaul. Other diesel locomotives on view at this, the north end of the shed, were a couple of English Electric Type 4's and one of the diesel mechanical 0-6-0 shunters, No.11159, which became D2240 in September 1960 and was later classified 04 under the TOPS scheme. The little 0-6-0DM had started life at Vulcan Foundry in June 1956 and its first shed had been New England. Note that the ancient northlight roof still has a lot of glass in place. *BLP - DB2992.*

One of the joys of Crewe South engine shed, especially for enthusiasts living north and east of Crewe, was the continual selection of former Great Western locomotives which stabled at the shed. The Western Region had their own small depot just over the Salop lines from 5B but that was only a two-road affair and would often fill up to capacity especially when a couple of 'Halls' or 'Granges' were resident. Any number WR locomotives from six to ten could be stabled on most days. Collett 2-8-0 No.3815 of Croes Newydd shed in Wrexham was a visitor to South shed in March 1960 and is under the coaler. This engine had recently given up employment in South Wales and was to spend the rest of its time, up to withdrawal in May 1964, working from Wrexham. The new paint around the front end signifies that the 2-8-0 had recently been to Wolverhampton Works for a minor overhaul or casual repair after accident damage. Engine cleaners were getting a bit thin on the ground by now. *BLP - DB2993.*

Even in April 1964 Western Region engines kept up their daily visits to Crewe. steam locomotives would go to the South shed whilst main line diesel hydraulic locomotives, both B-B 'Warships' and C-C 'Westerns', working in on trains from the West of England and South Wales, would gravitate to Crewe North shed. 'Grange' No.6860 ABERPORTH GRANGE was a rare visitor from Bristol St Philips Marsh shed and it was still wearing nameplates. In the background was another, unidentified member of the class whilst to its right the 'Grange' was rubbing shoulders with resident 'Jinty' No.47445. The latter locomotive was sold after it was withdrawn in 1966. Today, after many years working in the coal industry it has managed to reach preservation and is one of the few ex LMS 0-6-0T to survive. No.6860 was not so lucky as it entered Swindon Works in February 1965 and was broken up a few weeks later. *BLP - DB6699.*

Aston based 'Britannia' No.70005 JOHN MILTON was not looking its best in April 1964 when photographed at Crewe South along with an unidentified 0-6-0 tank. The unlikely pair were awaiting entry to the Works, the big engine for overhaul and the little un' for the chop more like. Note the Pacific still has nameplates in situ (see also *Steam Motive Power Centres No.1 - Doncaster*). By this time Crewe Works was only overhauling steam locomotives from the BR Standard classes, LMS Class 2, 5 and 8F's and some lucky 'Jubilees' although in most cases concerning this latter class only intermediate or casual repairs were handed out. Any other steam locomotive entering the premises would be on a one way journey to the scrapping shed. *BLP - DB6700.*

In March 1960 when Don Beecroft photographed 'Royal Scot' No.46116 IRISH GUARDSMAN at Crewe South shed, the 4-6-0 was allocated to Crewe North having transferred there in October 1958 from Camden. However, it was time for the 7P to report to the Works for overhaul, its last major repair before withdrawal in September 1963. Also in the Works line at 5B was Stanier 8F No.48131 from Rugby. The eight-coupled engine had spent much of its life on the Midland Division of the LMS, starting at Holbeck in 1941. Later it worked from Normanton, Toton, Wellingborough and finally Kettering before transferring to the Western Division at Rugby in October 1957. It was to spend the rest of its days in the latter Division and moved to Northampton in November 1960, Birkenhead in November 1962, Mold Junction in July 1963, Crewe South in January 1964 and finally Stoke in June 1964. Withdrawn in June 1967, it was purchased for scrap by Cashmores at Great Bridge in October of that year. The 'Scot' had nothing like as much time left to work. transferring to Edge Hill in October 1961, it moved on to Kingmoor in October 1962. just under a year later it returned to Crewe for a much needed overhaul but was instead condemned and scrapped there in September 1963, one of 15 of the class to disappear that year. *BLP - DB2995.*

'Jubilee' No.45741 LEINSTER shows off its tender to good measure in this rear three-quarter view at Crewe South shed in March 1960. Note the three plates affixed to the rear panel of the riveted tender. These plates informed of, from top to bottom: The number of the tender, the makers plate and at the bottom, the water capacity of the tender. Some of the Standard LMS tenders only had two plates affixed, the makers plate being left off. An Upperby engine since the previous November, this 4-6-0 had spent much of its BR life at Bushbury shed and was one of their six star performing 'Jubilees'. In July 1962 Kingmoor shed became its home for the next eighteen months but having becoming unserviceable whilst on a job to Motherwell in January 1964, No.45741 was withdrawn at 66B during the following February but in March, for some reason, it was taken to Crewe Works for cutting up. At that time nearby Cowlairs Works was busy scrapping anything which passed through its doors so another 'Jubilee' could have joined the other nine which had recently been scrapped there. Also, within a fifteen mile radius of Motherwell shed were a number of private scrapyards which were purchasing everything they could from BR, especially locomotives like a copper ridden 'Jubilee'. It still makes one think why such a long journey was undertaken by a withdrawn locomotive, towed more than two hundred miles. More than likely the scrap generated by LEINSTER was sent by train to one of the steel plants in Scotland. In the background, sheltering under the skeletal roof of the shed we can make out 'Jinty' No.47516, a local lad which used to attend derby works for overhaul. Its next visit to that establishment was some time off yet - February 1962 - but it was one-way trip. *BLP - DB2996.*

25

THE STATION

Getting underway after its scheduled stop at Crewe's platform 4, Edge Hill 'Princess Royal' No.46203 PRINCESS MARGARET ROSE, departs with an Up Liverpool express for London Euston in March 1960. By now the station is festooned with overhead catenary, the route to Manchester fully energised at 25kV a.c. Electric locomotives and multiple units are doing the job which until a few years previously had been the 'bread and butter' of steam motive power. The Liverpool route too was ready for its 'switch on' but until then the exLMS Pacifics allocated to Edge Hill shed would continue working these express trains through from Liverpool to London. As an important railway junction, Crewe station enjoyed a superb and varied train service. Without changing trains it was possible to travel from Crewe direct to Inverness, Glasgow, Edinburgh, Stranraer, York, Leeds, Holyhead, Swansea, Cardiff, Bristol, Bath, Plymouth, Penzance, Torquay, Bournemouth, Brighton, London, Birmingham, Derby, Manchester, Liverpool, Blackpool, and a host of other towns and cities in between. Admitted, some of the trains which gave those direct connections called at Crewe during the late small hours but nevertheless the choice was there. The station has changed somewhat since 1960, the layout has been simplified and non-stop trains pass through Crewe doing the magic 'ton' all day long but it is still an important junction and connections can still be made to virtually anywhere. *BLP - DB2986.*

Looking resplendent and well turned-out by the 8A cleaners, the 'Princess' heads south beneath the myriad of overhead cables but no matter - once south of Crewe the catenary will be left behind for now. Previously allocated to Crewe North shed, the Pacific moved to Liverpool in October 1958 and except for a few weeks in August 1960, it graced 8A until moving, for the purpose of being stored, to Carnforth in March 1961. Later that year, in July, it returned briefly to traffic Crewe North but went back to Carnforth in September where once again it was put into storage. On 24th January 1962 it was sent to Upperby where work was found over the next few months but then in April Kingmoor depot got hold of it and, after using it for most of the summer, they too put 46203 into storage. Withdrawn on 20th October 1962 the future for this lady looked grim. However, this engine was, of course, one of the lucky ones and it entered preservation after lying neglected at Carlisle Kingmoor during the winter of 1962-63. Note the Engineers saloon in the background. Now that was one busy vehicle during the electrification of the Manchester and Liverpool routes and the later schemes which took the catenary south to Stafford and beyond. *BLP - DB2985.*

(above) **Later that day in March 1960, Longsight based 'Royal Scot' No.46137 THE PRINCE OF WALE'S VOLUNTEERS SOUTH LANCASHIRE was another Up express using platform 4. The train is the Manchester -London (Euston) which should have started from London Road station but instead originated from Victoria/Exchange because of the engineering works associated with the electrification and the rebuilding of London Road station.. This 'Scot' had the second longest name in the class after No.46121 although up to 1949 No.46121 carried an abbreviated version of its later full name - H.L.I. Watching the progress of the 7P are the crew of Aston based 'Jubilee' No.45647 STURDEE which is waiting for a Birmingham (New Street) bound train to arrive from the north which they will then take forward to its destination.** *(right)* **As No.46137 finds its way through the numerous points and crossovers at the south end of the station, a track maintenance gang prepare to stand back and allow its passage. The constant coming and going of trains at Crewe must have been frustrating for these track gangs but at least they did not have to put up with goods trains as they used the deviation routes beneath the north end junctions. No.46137 transferred to Newton Heath shed in May 1960, its time wasting and track occupying journey from Longsight shed to Victoria station, and the return, being seen for what it was. In January 1961 the 'Scot' moved to Trafford Park shed, again to work London bound trains but from Manchester (Central) to London (St Pancras) this time. Derby got it five months later then Saltley in August. The end came at Carlisle Upperby during the mass cull of October 1962. Crewe Works scrapped the engine in May 1963.** *BLP - DB3137 & 3138.*

Another Liverpool express waits to journey south to Euston in March 1960 but this time from platform 5 and with different motive power in the shape of 'Rebuilt Patriot' No.45529 STEPHENSON. This was a Crewe North engine so it may have come on to the train here but the coal in the tender suggests that No.45529 has already put about thirty miles or so under its belt. The tender previously coupled behind a 'Jubilee' was one of the 4000 gallon Mk.II Stanier welded type acquired in July 1947 by this engine at rebuilding. It kept the same tender No.9767, to withdrawal. From its rebuild, STEPHENSON had swapped between Camden and Crewe North depots on a regular basis but the latter shed had hold of it for by far the longest time. To break the previous link Willesden shed was the recipient of this engine in January 1961 and they kept hold of it for more than two and half years, including a two month spell at the former North London Railway depot at Devons Road shed, in store. During October 1963, in the company of a handful of unwanted and run-down 'Scots', the 'Patriot' broke new ground and was transferred to Annesley shed on the former Great Central main line for working the Nottingham (Victoria) Marylebone semi-fast expresses. It didn't last long at Annesley and in February 1964, having worked more than one and a half million revenue miles it went into Crewe Works for scrapping. *BLP - DB3139.*

The date is June 1958 and one of Wellingborough's Crosti equipped 9F 2-10-0s, No.92024, stands in the yard at Crewe Works ready to return home after overhaul. Being built at Crewe, these strange beasts were familiar fare to the fitters in the shops although those double barrel boilers must have proved to be difficult to maintain. Built in June 1955, No.92024 spent its early years at 15A both as a fundamental Crosti and a conventional engine after conversion. After being less than successful, the Crosti concept was judged to be a failure and all the class were converted to conventional types between September 1959 and July 1962. Getting rid of the second boiler gave these London Midland Region 9F's a new lease of life and all of them, except No.92028 withdrawn in October 1966, worked to the end of 1967, outliving many of their conventional cousins in the process. No.92024 ended up at Birkenhead (didn't they all it seems) in July 1965 and was condemned at that depot in November 1967. 'Unrebuilt Patriot' No.45551 from Upperby shed stands behind waiting to enter the Paint Shop. *BLP - DB765.*

31

(opposite) 'Royal Scot' No.46100 ROYAL SCOT outside the Erecting Shop South in April 1959. Marked up for the erecting shop staff, the engine appears to have just received an overhaul and is now waiting for a tow to the paint shop after coupling up to its tender en route. This tenderless view of the engine gives us a good look at the cab interior and the coupling arrangements below the footplate. The wire hawser was used to haul the dead engine out of the shops into the yard where any last minute adjustments could be carried out, space inside the shop being very much at a premium even with the vast workforce employed here. Note that there is no sidescreen fitted on this side of the cab, only the driver having the benefit of that particular aid. *(above)* In the next but one line to the right of 46100, another of the class, No.46154 THE HUSSAR is in the same state and which gives us a glance at the right side of the cab. Note the left side cab window is broken but the sidescreen is intact. Note also that in both pictures the yard is festooned with all sorts of equipment and rubbish although some kind of order prevails judging by the carefully stacked trolleys and pipe racks. Both of these 'Scots' were allocated to Camden shed at the time when these views were captured but once the summer timetable of 1959 was concluded the pair parted company with 46100 transferring to Nottingham shed until October 1962 when withdrawal took place. Fittingly it was acquired by a most unusual private buyer and eventually reached preservation. One wonders, in view of its early retirement in 1962, along with twenty-eight other members of the class, if ROYAL SCOT would have been saved for posterity had not that enterprising purchaser seen its potential. No.46154 had a less settled ending. From Camden it transferred to Preston followed by stints at Edge Hill, Willesden, Llandudno Junction, Holyhead and finally Willesden again before being condemned in November 1962. It entered Crewe Works during the following March for scrapping. *BLP - DB1415 & 1416.*

Two more 'Scots' visiting the works in April 1959 were No.46164 THE ARTISTS RIFLEMAN *(opposite)* and No.46121 HIGHLAND LIGHT INFANTRY, CITY OF GLASGOW REGIMENT *(above)*. The former was positioned on the same road as No.46100 and to its left is a Class 5 which has also just been wheeled out of the Erecting Shop wearing a coat of primer. No.46164 was the last of the 'Scots featured on these four pages to be rebuilt and acquire the 2A boiler, fitted in 1951. An Edge Hill engine at the time of this photograph, it probably had the most inglorious career ending amongst the featured group. Reallocating to Crewe North in September 1959, it moved to Millhouses in February 1960 but when that shed closed it was sent to Canklow, a depot with no history of having express passenger engines within its roundhouse. Finally, with appropriate work difficult to find for such an engine in the Sheffield District it was moved to Darnall shed in June 1962. At an establishment more used to dealing with Robinson, Gresley and Thompson designed engines, the 'Royal Scot' had no place - it was a bad time for any steam locomotive but if you happened to be a 'foreigner' the future was grim. Inevitably, during the following December, withdrawal took place and No.46164 at least had the benefit of a decent funeral being towed to Crewe Works for breaking up. No.46121 was a Polmadie engine, and in this view, after a visit to the Paint Shop, it looks superb with even the three plates on the rear of the 4000 gallon tender, No.9361, painted and legible. This particular 'Scot' qualified as having the longest nameplate in the class, in terms of the number of letters and characters, and to top off that nameplate was a Regimental badge which can be seen in this view. However, up to 1949 it had what was the shortest nameplate where the abbreviation H.L.I. was used. Not having been given the same adoration from the painters, an unidentified Stanier 8F is also ready to go back into traffic. *BLP - DB1417 & 1420.* 35

I can't ever remember if it has been pointed out to me or if anyone has ever published the fact but note that every steam locomotive which visited Crewe Works for repair entered the place with smokebox facing west. Those coming in for scrapping could be facing east or west it did not matter. The reasons why west was the right way was because it just made everything so much easier for all concerned and besides the works was not equipped with a turntable of any kind. So when tenders were detached, repaired, and ready to be coupled up again with a locomotive, it could be any locomotive theoretically because locomotives and tenders were all facing the same way. Crewe South shed had the job of assembling the locomotives attending Works and if necessary they could turn whole lines of engines to face the right way in one go by taking them around the triangle of lines formed by the Salop and Basford Hall lines. More than likely individual engines were turned as required before they were put into groups on the Works lines at 5B. Inside the Works back in April 1959, we have already seen a handful of 'Scots', even No.46121 gets a nose into this view over the Vacuum Pits but Pacific No.46257 CITY OF SALFORD is the focus of the photographer. The Upperby 'Duchess', was apparently in the shops to receive AWS equipment, note the protection plate where the absent front coupling normally hangs. Also in the picture is the latterly preserved 'Jubilee' No.45593 KOLHAPUR, another Upperby charge recently fitted with AWS. *BLP - DB1421.*

In contradiction of the last caption and the west facing smokeboxes theory, 'Jubilee' No.45613 KENYA languishes in the works yard, near the Chester main line (behind the fence) in April 1959 and it is plainly facing eastwards! The only explanation I can give is that the engine had possibly been out on road testing or perhaps recently returned to its then home depot at Chester when something was found to the amiss. A quick return to works was ordered and it must have come in via the back door off the Chester line. Note the DO NOT MOVE board tucked away on the front end. Whatever the mechanical problem was, it must not have required the locomotive to go through the usual channels to enter the works. Shortly after its return to traffic No.45613 was reallocated to Crewe North shed in May and then later in the year to Edge Hill. Afterwards both the Crewe depots had its services then Carnforth got it in May 1962. Kingmoor shed was its last home where, in September 1964, it was withdrawn. In the background, under the gantry crane Cl.5 No.44761 has a red flag attached to the tender bufferbeam. The tender is also full of coal - perhaps it too was a casualty requiring some after overhaul maintenance? At least it is facing the 'right' way. *BLP - DB1414.*

Former Wolverton Carriage Works shunter CD6 *(above)* presents a sorry sight whilst its awaits the call to the scrapping line at Crewe Works in April 1959. Its chimney prodigious chimney is missing, assumed to have been the result of accident but no matter because it will not be required any more. Sister engine CD7 did at least mange to keep its chimney to the end and is seen *(opposite)* outside the Paint Shop at Crewe in the March of 1960. CD7 was the last of its line - Ramsbottom's LNWR Special Tanks. Dating from 1870, there were still more than 230 of them at Grouping even though withdrawals had started in 1913. However, the LMS got rid of many during the 1920's, especially those which had not been rebuilt from the original sloping front design, with smokebox doors which opened upwards. The last engine in the Running Stock fleet, 27423, was withdrawn in 1941 but those in the Service Stock fleet such as the four at Wolverton: CD1, CD2, CD6 and CD7 lasted well into the BR era. One engine in Departmental service No.3323 still had that number (its original LNW number) in 1949 and was renumbered 43323 until it was realised that it duplicated the ex Midland Johnson 0-6-0 so the LNW 0-6-0ST reverted back to being simply 3323. CD7 is seen here in the company of the 0-4-0 tram engine which had been a fixture of the Paint Shop for many years. *BLP - DB1413 & 2998.*

Now here is a little corner of what might be termed 'Stanierland'. Its still April 1959 and we are still in the yard at Crewe Works - where else could this be? 'Princess' No.46203 PRINCESS MARGARET ROSE, of Crewe North shed, dominates the picture with two Midland Division 'Jubilees' Nos.45616 MALTA G.C. of Kentish Town shed and 45650 BLAKE of Nottingham shed filling the background along with a filthy, unidentified 8F. All the, by now, tenderless engines are awaiting their turn to visit the Erecting Shop which, if this was a Sunday, will be attained by all of them by about Wednesday. *BLP - DB1412.*

Still wearing the old British Railways emblem in April 1959, Crewe North 'Jubilee' No.45674 DUNCAN is outside the Paint Shop ready for a fresh coat of paint and the new crest. Work has already started prior to the weekend break and the wheels have been chocked. Come Monday morning, weather permitting, and this engine would be swarming with men rubbing down its external surfaces prior to undercoating. The AWS protection plate appears new, perhaps 45674's visit to works was for the fitting of the warning equipment and the opportunity arose for the application of paint and new insignia. *BLP - DB1423.*

In March 1960 Longsight 'Jubilee' No.45671 PRINCE RUPERT had undergone a complete overhaul (Heavy General) and, ex Erecting Shop, it is paired up with its tender outside the Paint Shop ready for its last ever painting which will see it through to withdrawal in November 1963 when it next visited Crewe Works for major surgery. By then it would have moved on from Manchester, going first to Llandudno Junction in September 1960, ousted out of Longsight by the growing band of English Electric Type 4 diesels and the a.c. electrics. In June 1961 Crewe North had its services for five months before its final transfer took it to Warrington's Dallam shed, a depot not normally associated with 'namers' of any class but by the early 1960's anything and everything was possible on BR. To the left of the 4-6-0 is one of the many ex LMS tank locomotives maintained at Crewe. This one is Bangor's Class 4 No.42674 which was an early candidate for withdrawal. It was another victim of the mass cull carried out in late 1962 when it was allocated to Stoke shed. Derby Works carried out the breaking up process. *BLP - DB3101.*

Nicely turned out push&pull fitted Ivatt Class 2 tank No.41288 from Sutton Oak shed is nearly ready to return home in March 1960. Note the use of the old BR emblem on the tank side - an acute shortage of the smaller version of the 1956 crest must have been the reason for that being applied. Having moved to Dallam shed in April 1961, this 2-6-2T was another victim of the winter cull of 1962 and would visit Crewe Works one more time, in March 1963, for breaking up. *BLP - DB3102.*

Kentish Town based 'Scot' No.46103 ROYAL SCOTS FUSILIER appears ready to leave works and head back to the Midland main line in March 1960. This engine was one of the early participants of the LMS 'Royal Scot' rebuilding programme, receiving its 2A taper boiler in 1943 after which it left the Western Division for a new life on the Midland Division at Leeds Holbeck, a depot which kept hold of it until late 1958 when Kentish Town was the recipient. By the summer of 1961 the writing was on the wall for the 'Scots'. Ancient by any standards, even in rebuilt form, they had run their 30 year economic life expectancy but worse than that they were clapped-out. The authorities started to send them to any depot where useful work might be found but they were grasping at straws. RSF found itself at Saltley in June 1961 and miraculously hung around there for twelve months prior to going north to Upperby. They had no need for it and at the cessation of the summer timetable sent it back to Holbeck. Unwanted, No.46103 was laid-up, condemned in December 1962 and then stored for nine months at Farnley Junction shed. The call from Crewe came in September 1963 and the fallen giant was put out of its misery. Note the absence of AWS which at that period was not installed on the Midland lines. The Stanier Class 5, No.45371 of Upperby shed, would visit works again and be given another repaint before its end came in April 1967 when allocated to Workington. From new in June 1937, the Cl.5 had been allocated to Llandudno Junction depot and except for a three month loan to Holyhead later that year, the engine resided at 6G until July 1945 when Willesden got it. Two years later a transfer to Upperby would see the engine work out its days in the north-west of England. Down by the Paint shop is the former LNW Special Tank CD7. *BLP - DB3103.*

One of the nice things about visiting any locomotive works was the surprise element, and occasionally the shock of seeing a particular perhaps favourite locomotive being cut up. The former is represented here at Crewe in March 1960 by 'Coronation' No.46249 CITY OF SHEFFIELD coupled, or at least appearing to be coupled, to a former LNWR tender. The marriage looks wholly inappropriate and one wonders just how far the big engine would get if such a coupling had ever taken place. Luckily locomotive engineers kept up with the evolution of tenders alongside their quest for larger and more powerful engines. Another striking aspect of this picture is the filth clinging to the Pacific. Considering these engines were the top flight motive power of the LMR, even in 1960, it is amazing that so much grime was allowed to accumulate on the engine. Perhaps Crewe North shed, the home of 46249 at the time, was short of cleaners, who knows. By coincidence the engine is stood opposite the cleaning pits where engines were given a good wash and degrease prior to entering the Erecting Shop. Maybe SHEFFIELD' had not progressed that far yet in the Crewe Works scheme. *BLP - DB3106.*   45

Crewe Works could be relied upon to produce a reasonable number of Pacifics amongst its gathering and this particular Sunday in March 1960 was no exception. 'Princess' No.46201 PRINCESS ELIZABETH is seen here rubbing shoulders with a 'Duchess' whilst lesser mortals surround them. Note that the Polmadie Pacific has yet to have AWS fitted and it was probably during this 'shopping' that it was put on. Just on the right of the picture is the cab of one of the BR-built Stanier Class 5's, No.44692. Ex Horwich Works in October 1950, it was a long time resident of Bank Hall shed but moved to Accrington in November 1955. In March 1961 it moved to Rose Grove and in June of that year to Southport. In March 1962 Aintree became home for fourteen months when it then went north for its first stint at Kingmoor shed. In July 1964 Lostock Hall got it but 44692 returned to 12A in October. Withdrawal took place in May 1966 and after a short period in store at Kingmoor it ended its days at a scrapyard in Shettleston, Glasgow. The LNW 0-8-0 behind The 'Lizzie' was one of a number still receiving overhauls at Crewe, unidentified here, the G2a was possibly amongst the following receiving repairs at that time: 49081, 49120, 49142, 49267, 49328 and 49439. *BLP - DB3107.*

Unrebuilt Patriots were also receiving repairs in March 1960, the first withdrawals being some months away. Upperby's No.45524 BLACKPOOL still has its tender attached and has just gone through the washing and degreasing process. Notice the pile of muck at the end of the hard standing to the right. In the background is our old friend No.46249 and the bizarre tender combination seen from another angle - it still looks wrong. No.45524 moved to Warrington Dallam in the September after this works visit, then on 10th June 1961 to Edge Hill but there was no hiding place for these old timers. On the 15th September 1962, at Crewe Works, the inevitable took place - having covered more than one and a quarter million revenue miles and just 29 years old - No.45524 was withdrawn. 1962 was a bad year for the 'Patriot' class with twenty-five condemnations. Add on the two withdrawn in late 1960 along with the nine from 1961 and the class looks suddenly on the verge of annihilation. All except two of those thirty-six engines were cut up at Crewe, the odd men out were 45507 and 45518 which were dealt with at Horwich. However not all the casualties were unrebuilt engines. No.45514 HOLYHEAD, rebuilt in March 1947, was condemned 27th May 1961 whilst 45536 PRIVATE W. WOOD V.C., rebuilt in November 1948, was withdrawn 29th December 1962. Both of those early 'rebuilt' casualties had been involved for a short time with Sheffield area sheds right up to their demise! *BLP - DB3105.*

After more than twenty-five years working from Western Division sheds, 'Patriot' No.45519 LADY GODIVA moved onto the old Midland Division into what was then Great Western territory or to be more official - BR (Western Region). Its new home was Bristol Barrow Road depot, the old Midland roundhouse located about a mile north of Temple Meads station. That was in November 1958 and now, in March 1960, the engine has returned to its old haunts, or at least its main workshop, for its last overhaul. The 'Lady' is ready to return south and appears to have all the necessary equipment. Note the screw couplings stacked up alongside what was the Vacuum Pits, the final stage in the steam locomotive overhaul process at Crewe Works. Just peeping into the picture is Nottingham based Cl.5 No.45234 which, ended up at Newton Heath shed in February 1966 and lasted nearly to the end of steam being withdrawn in September 1967. *BLP - DB3110.*

At the end of World War Two it was the intention of the LMS authorities to rebuild eighteen of the Patriot class with taper boilers and for them to be rated at 6P standard against the 5XP of the original engines. In the event that is exactly what happened with the rebuilding carried out over a four year period from 1946. The future of the rest of the class was to be decided later. When the question arose once again, during the early years of British Railways, it was decided that the unrebuilt Patriots would be withdrawn after they were replaced by the new lightweight Standard Pacifics (the 'Clans') of which at least twenty were planned for building initially. As history tells us, the number of 'Clans' only ever reached ten so the lives of the unrebuilt 'Patriots' was safe for the time being. Railway history would have been somewhat different had the pot of money given to BR been of the bottomless kind. Certainly, the other 'Clans' would have been built and possibly more of the 'Patriots' would have been rebuilt but the pot was always running out and the authorities had to 'make do' sometimes hence the extended lives of the unrebuilt engines. No.45542, seen in the yard at Crewe Works in March 1960, along with 'Jubilee' No.45591, was one of the original or rather, unrebuilt 'Patriots'. The engine was in fact the first of the last batch ordered by the LMS, all ten being built at Crewe and put into traffic between 13th March and 2nd May 1934. When the unrebuilt 'Patriots' were withdrawn it was because they were due new boilers, the rest of the engine being deemed, apparently, in good condition. However, dieselisation was, by 1962, becoming the priority on BR. Virtually nothing of what precious little money was available was to be spent on steam traction. So, by 1960 Preston based No.45542 was living on a knife edge. In July 1961 it transferred to Nuneaton, its days on express passenger trains now gone forever, but even at Nuneaton suitable work was hard to come by and in November it was sent for storage at Rugby shed along with Nos.45537, 45538, 45541, 45544 and 45548. Whilst in ' serviceable' store it was withdrawn in June 1962 and by September it was in the Scrap Shop at Crewe. *BLP - DB3111.*

On their way to the Paint Shop together, 'Jubilee' No.45591 UDIAPUR and the unnamed 'Patriot' No.45542 pause for the weekend in the works yard in March 1960. The Crewe North 'Jubilee' has gone through a full 'Heavy General' overhaul, probably its last, whilst 45542 appears to have had a lesser repair. In the event No.45591 outlived the other engine by about eighteen months. Except for a three month period at the beginning of 1935 spent on the Central Division, and a few weeks at Trafford Park in early 1956, this engine spent all of its career on the Western Lines, its last seven years being at 5A. This picture shows No.45591 in the pink primer associated with new locomotives rather than repaired examples. One wonders why the Erecting Shop would go to the trouble of painting an engine virtually all over when the Paint Shop was not too far away? *BLP - DB3108.*

(opposite) Is that a 'shopping list' chalked on the cabside of 'Jubilee' No.45655 KEITH seen outside Erecting Shop South in March 1960? It would have been nice to have got hold of a photograph of that list which most probably would tell us what had been done to this engine rather than what else was required to be done to it - who knows? For certain No.45655 has gone through a major overhaul and various parts which had been stripped off, for attention in other departments, have come back to the rightful owner. The major overhaul process at Crewe (Heavy General) would entail a locomotive entering the Erecting Shop minus its tender but otherwise complete. All of the running gear, underbody, frames and upper body would have been steam cleaned and degreased prior to entry. Once inside the shop the engine would be completely stripped down to frames, the boiler would go away for repair whilst another boiler would be waiting to take its place. All parts which were worn out would be replaced whilst other parts would be refurbished. Retyred wheels, complete with axles, would be fitted once the frame has been thoroughly repaired and painted. Cylinders will have been either rebored or replaced. Paint would have been applied to all areas which were inaccessible once the engine was completed. Wooden floorboards in the cab will also have been replaced. After about two weeks or less, the engine will emerge like KEITH here, ready for a trip to the Paint Shop, not forgetting to pick up a tender on the way. The BR locomotive works staff made it all appear so easy. Note the dazzle type camouflage still abiding to the Erecting Shop brickwork, some fifteen years after the ending of hostilities. Also, high on the gable, immediately above the locomotive, is the building date of this edifice to the steam locomotive. Long may the place survive. *BLP - DB3123.*

Two classic views of 'Jubilee' No.45555 QUEBEC in March 1960 after completing a major overhaul. *(above)* We can appreciate the near perfect symmetry between the engine and tender. In fact, from any angle this class of engine looked good with the Stanier 4000 gallon tender. This particular tender is one of the Mk II welded type, probably No.10365. Note that only two plates adorn the rear panel, the top one is the rectangular, combined maker's (LMS) and number plate, whilst lower oval one carries the capacity information. At this time in 1960 QUEBEC was allocated to Carlisle Upperby shed having arrived there from Bushbury in November 1959. In January 1961 the engine transferred to Crewe South shed where it was to finish its days in August 1963. No.45555 had in fact been laid up at 5B since May of that year but it was September before it was called into works for cutting up. Built at Crewe in 1934, the fourth engine of its order, it was not named until 1937, long after the rest of the class had been completed. *BLP - DB3112.*

52

This view of 'Jubilee' No.45639 RALEIGH outside Erecting Shop South in March 1960 gives us a fleeting view of the new outside traverser which was being installed. What kind of headaches did the building of that equipment cause during the installation period? The Holbeck based engine has been given a new coat of Brunswick green paint and full lining. However, where the painting process was carried out is unknown but looking at the probable disruption appertaining at the time, a section of the erecting shop was possibly used for the purpose. No.45639 still requires AWS to be fitted but was its usual hunting grounds yet equipped? Perhaps the 'Jubilee' was never fitted with AWS. It did work out its final days from Holbeck shed, being withdrawn in October 1963. It came back to Crewe and was broken up here in January 1964. Across on the east side of the new traverser pit is a Willesden based Fairburn Cl.4 2-6-4T No.42234, which has also undergone major overhaul and is ready to return south to put in four more years work before withdrawal. This particular tank engine was laid up at Willesden shed for most of 1964 and for some unknown reason it was broken up on site in November of that year, obviously deemed unfit to travel. *BLP - DB3124*.

Further down the yard that day, on one of the Paint Shop roads, 'another 'Jubilee', No.45666 CORNWALLIS was ready to got back into traffic at Crewe North. Note that besides its own screw coupling the engine also sports a three-link job from one of the Works shunters. Note also that the tender is still adorned with the old British Railways lion and wheel emblem, nearly four years after it was superseded by the new crest. AWS equipment has been fitted and it was probably that work which brought the engine into shops. It is difficult to discern if the paint is new or has the locomotive simply had a good steam cleaning. *BLP - DB3113.*

Ready for the Erecting Shop in April 1964, 'Jubilee' No.45647 STURDEE is one of the lucky members of the by now greatly diminished class. Whilst other 'Jubilees' were being cut up, both here and at other BR works, No.45647 was getting ready for a new lease of life in the North Eastern Region at Farnley Junction depot. When new in January 1935, this engine was allocated to Crewe North, but later moved to Rugby thereafter it was constantly associated with 5A, as were many of its class. In 1953 it transferred to Bushbury where it settled down for seven years working into Euston on the expresses from Wolverhampton. In February 1960 Aston got hold of it for a couple of years and they too used the engine on similar workings. In June 1962 it returned to Crewe North who sent it off to Saltley nine months later. Now that transfer should have sealed the engine's fate but by some good fortune it survived Saltley shed and returned for a final stint at Crewe North. As if getting rid of a hot potato, 5A immediately sent STURDEE off to Farnley Junction where, for the next three years it survived to become one of the final eight operational 'Jubilees'. Withdrawn in April 1967 at Leeds Holbeck shed, it was moved for storage purposes to Wakefield shed in the summer and was purchased for scrap by Cashmore's at Great Bridge in September. In the background Ivatt Cl.2 No.46436 from Bury and 8F No.48053 from Coalville await their turn for overhaul. *BLP - DB6689.*

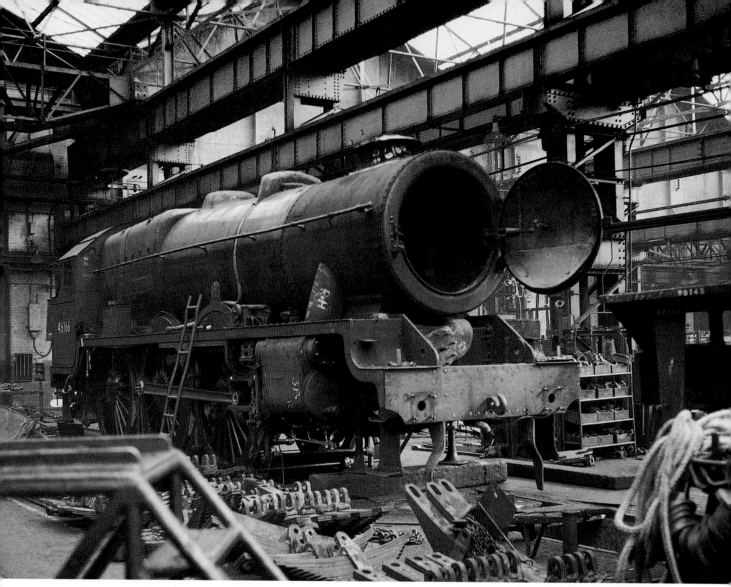

Inside Erecting Shop South (No.10) in March 1960, amongst about sixty-odd other locomotives, was this 'Royal Scot' No.46166 LONDON RIFLE BRIGADE. It is now being put back together after being stripped down to its frame. By the middle of the week it will be hauled outside ready for a trip to the Paint Shop. Besides all the steam locomotives under repair in these shops, there was another production line, two in fact, building new diesel locomotives. These lines were to be found in the south bay i.e. those nearest the Chester line. The diesel locomotives being built at the time of this photograph were the last of a batch of BR Sulzer Type 2 Bo-Bo's (D5076-D5093) and the first lot of BR Sulzer Type 4's (D68-D137). A batch of 0-6-0 diesel-electric shunters in the D38XX number range were being built in yet another shop. Such was the capacity of Crewe. In December 1958 Crewe had built its last steam locomotive, BR Standard 9F No.92250. The last steam locomotive repair would be given to another Crewe product, 'Britannia' No.70013 OLIVER CROMWELL in February 1967. Over 8,000 locomotives were built at Crewe, more than 7,300 were steam. The number of steam locomotives receiving overhauls apparently numbered about 125,000. Those locomotives broken up must be approaching or perhaps exceeding the number built there. 57
BLP - DB3119.

March 1960. No.10 Shop. 'Coronation' No.46246 CITY OF MANCHESTER has gone through a 'General' and, at last, has also got rid of the last remnants of its former streamlined casing, the sloping top to the smokebox. It would appear that lubrication lines are the next priority in the refitting process. The partially undressed Pacific reveals the two inside cylinders, or at least their covers, which are normally covered when in service. Note the lifting strops and shackles hanging from the overhead crane hook above the 8F. *BLP - DB3118.*

Here is a 'Scot' put back together and nice and shiny although it is still to be coupled to its intended tender. No.46114 COLDSTREAM GUARDSMAN was an Edge Hill engine, used to hard work on the heavy expresses hauled between Liverpool and London - a fitting employment for a proud powerful locomotive. However, such was the cessation of steam traction on BR and the seemingly manic introduction of new diesel and electric locomotives, many of these 7P express locomotives ended up in places they were never intended to go nor work some of the traffic they did. There was no dignified end during the early 60's. In December 1960 No.46114 was transferred to Willesden but they sent it to Bushbury six weeks later. In June it was moved to Llandudno Junction and then Holyhead at the end of the timetable in September. It managed to keep a foothold on Anglesey until June 1963 when Willesden was chosen to house it again. They had no requirement for it so sent it to Annesley in September 1963 but it apparently never got to the Nottinghamshire depot on the old GC route or if it did they sent it right beck to London because it was condemned that month and was stored until February 1964 when it went north once again but this time to the Slag Reduction Co., at Rotherham. *BLP - DB3104.*

G2 class No.49404 of Edge Hill shed had just completed its last overhaul at Crewe in March 1960 and is looking resplendent in unlined black livery, complete with the new BR crest on its tender. This engine had spent most of its BR life allocated to the Merseyside depot, an establishment which specialised in keeping the former LNW 0-8-0 tender engines. When 49404 was ready for home, 8A still had about twenty 0-8-0 of classes G2 and G2a on its books. Only Springs Branch could muster more, into the mid twenties. Within Lancashire as a whole most of the class must have resided by early 1960. The depots concerned being Longsight, Patricroft, Preston, Speke Junction, Sutton Oak besides those previously mentioned. Note the apparently newly created cab extension on the tender, handy for those winter months or inclement weather tender first running. Such niceties, or 'Back cabs' as the LNW enginemen called them, were introduced about 1915 but they were still being fitted on the tenders into BR days. The rear sandbox fillers have been moved from the cab floor to the cab side for easier access. This 0-8-0 came back to Crewe Works once more, in May 1962, when it was condemned and then cut up. *BLF*

- *DB3115.*

Up until the inauguration of the Manchester-Crewe electrification, and the upgrading of the main line from Manchester to Stoke-on-Trent, 'Britannia' No.70043 LORD KITCHENER had been allocated to Longsight shed for most of its short life. A regular on the Manchester (London Road)-London (Euston) expresses via Stoke where, up until the mid-1950's, even 'Royal Scots' were banned because of their axle loading. The Longsight Pacifics, with their reduced overall weight and extra set of wheels were ideal for the job. Manchester-London expresses which travelled via Crewe did not have that problem and so 'Scots', 'Lizzies' and sometimes 'Duchesses' could be used without fear of upsetting the Civil Engineer. 9A shed had five regular 'Brits' for the express work, Nos.70031, 70032, 70033, 70043 and 70044, with others which came and went during the period December 1952 to September 1961. In March 1960, less than seven years since the Pacific was wheeled out of these shops and into the open air for the first time, No.70043 was paying a visit to its birthplace for what appears to be a minor overhaul. This engine was one of two 'Brits' involved in the coal train acceleration and braking tests on the Midland main line in 1953/54. Along with 70044, which was similarly decked out with Westinghouse braking equipment in place of the usual smoke deflectors they performed for many months on that line, being variously allocated to Toton or Derby for the purpose. When the tests were concluded both the 'Brits' returned to Crewe to have the Westinghouse gear removed and have their smoke deflectors and nameplates fitted. When not involved in the brake testing, both 70043 and 70044 worked the London expresses from Manchester, complete with Westinghouse pumps but otherwise anonymous. In front of LORD KITCHENER is another Crewe product, BR Standard 9F No.92086 which has also just emerged from No.10 Shop. *BLP - DB3121.*

61

Likewise, 'Brit' No.70051 FIRTH OF FORTH has also emerged from No.10 Shop after what seems to have been a more intensive overhaul. Note that the cab extension frame is still to be put back on, otherwise all is complete. The Polmadie Pacific was built here in 1954, entering traffic in August. All of the LMR based 'Brits' along with those resident in Scotland, came to Crewe for overhauls. Doncaster looked after the Eastern Region allocation whilst Swindon did the same for the Western Region batch. In front of 70051 stands one of the ubiquitous WD Austerity 2-8-0s, No.90527 of Aintree shed. *BLP - DB3122.*

During the decade covering the 1950's, Crewe Works had an eclectic assortment of shunting engines which kept the place moving. One of those engines in April 1959 was this ex Caledonian 'Pug' 0-4-0ST No.56027, wearing its works identification W10 and a coating of coal on its cab roof June 1958. There was basically no escape from this place once a locomotive was 'signed in' but there was exceptions. Withdrawn in October 1960, the little four-coupled tank, built to a Caley design dating back to 1878, was stored at the works until February 1961 when a slot was found for it inside the scrapping shop. *BLP - DB1419.*

April 1959. Ex Lanky 'A' class No.52312 *(opposite)* which had been rebuilt with a Belpaire firebox and extended smokebox, a conversion which somewhat spoilt the original no nonsense looks. However, they too undertook much of the towing, pushing, toing and froing and other requirements of a works shunter at Britain's largest locomotive works. This is the Flag Lane location and immediately behind the 'A' class is 0-6-0ST No.51444 *(above)*. Beyond that, near the bridge are a couple of ex LMS 4F 0-6-0s, Nos.44373 and 44374. No.52312 had been at Crewe since December 1953, ex Bolton shed. 51412, 51444, 51446, 52093, 52201, 52207, 52212, 52218, 52225, 52312, 52345, 52441, 52459, 52464, 52517. Why the 'A' class was such a popular engine for the shunting gang at Crewe Works is a mystery to this writer but nevertheless most of them ended their working days at the place and were scrapped there. However, when it came down to overhauls for these engines, they all made the trip to Horwich and then returned to Crewe. Some did get away from Crewe. No.52207 left its employment at the works and transferred to Crewe South shed in September 1958 and from there it made its way back to L&Y territory in August 1959, ending up at Bury and finally it went to Lees in January 1960. No.52201 was another 'A' class which escaped the clutches of Crewe. Arriving at Crewe in February 1958, ex Sutton Oak, it left for Patricroft during the following July. No.52225 had a stint at the works from May to August 1958 when it went back from whence it came - Warrington Dallam. No.52345 also did a vanishing act in 1958 after more than four years in residence. The LMS 3F 0-6-0T was another class which congregated in strength at Crewe Works for shunting purposes although many of those arrived in the early 60's as replacements for withdrawn L&Y engines. 47330, 47380, 47384, 47391, 47400, 47492, 47494, 47505, 47592, 47597, 47608, 47615, 47618, 47646, 47658, 47661. During the early BR days ex LNWR engines took on the bulk of the work before the L&Y invasion of 1953. 2F 0-6-0 tender engines Nos.58321, 58323, 58326, 58328, 58332, 58336, 58343, and 58347 are known to have put in time at the works before their demise. The 0-4-2 saddletanks Nos.47862 and 47865 were shunting around the place till 1956 and 1953 respectively. North London Railway 0-6-0T No.58857 was tried during the summer of 1953 but returned to Devons Road in August. LMS 4F 0-6-0s Nos.44373 and 44374 arrived from Stoke as the heavyweights in July 1958. *BLP -* 65

DB1424 & 1425.

(opposite) **The fleet of works engines was a tidy one and at weekends they could be found stabled mainly alongside the boiler park on the old Stone Yard site at Flag Lane as seen in the previous illustrations but there were exceptions and nothing could be taken for granted. Ex Lanky 0-6-0ST No.51412 had been left on the Vacuum Pits during one weekend in April 1959. Note that there is no three-link coupling on the front drawhook but around this place couplings could be found virtually everywhere. A lone 'Jubilee' featured elsewhere in this album, can be seen outside the Paint Shop during a particularly quiet weekend around that department.** *BLP - DB1422.*

(above) **Getting more up-to-date with the Works steam locomotive shunter fleet: 3F 0-6-0T No.47597, carrying target No.9 in April 1964. Withdrawn in November 1965, this engine was sold for scrap to T.W.Wards at Killamarsh in January 1966. It was too late for the 3F tank to be cut up at Crewe - the scrapping of steam locomotives there had ceased.** *BLP - DB6692.*

Two more 'Britannia's' photographed in the works at Crewe by Don Beecroft were No.70010 OWEN GLENDOWER *(opposite)* and No.70022 TORNADO *(above)*. The date now is April 1964. Massive changes have occurred within the motive power community. The diesels and electrics are well established - they are here to stay. Crewe Works has now ceased doing any repairs to its wonderful Stanier Pacifics, in fact their time is nearly over, all the 'Lizzies' are gone and most of the 'Coronation' class are either scrapped or laid up. Only a couple of examples are still flying the flag and of those engines, they can get no better work than hauling fish, meat, parcels or empty stock trains with the occasional overnight postal or sleeper train duties. The 'Brits' will soon take over as the only Pacifics working on the London Midland Region but even their employment is being slowly demeaned as they are relegated to becoming stand-ins for failed diesels or working excursions, specials, extras, empty stock and goods, both fitted and unfitted. Times were bad for steam locomotives and were about to get worse. At least Willesden's No.70010 is getting something of a clean-up, but as for what repair has taken place the writer knows nothing. 70022, however, looks to be in a sorry state. Not only has the accumulated filth nearly obliterated its identity, the fall plate on the rear of the footplate appears rather bashed about as a result of what I'm not sure but the Pacific was sorted out and returned to Aston shed. Both of these engines ended up at Carlisle Kingmoor, 70010 keeping going until September 1967 whilst 70022 made it to the end of that year. *BLP - DB6687 & 6688.*

Two ex LNWR 0-8-0 G2a class engines which came into Crewe Works in March 1960 for breaking up were Nos.49378 from Springs Branch and 49327 from Bescot. Both had been withdrawn in November 1959, the former being laid up at the old Lancashire & Yorkshire shed in Wigan (27D), whilst 49327 had stayed put at Bescot awaiting the call to Crewe. No.49327 dated from October 1918 and was a relative youngster at 42 years compared with No.49378 which had just celebrated 57 years service to three different owners. Prior to working at Springs Branch, No.49378 had spent the war years at Plodder Lane, Farnworth and before that Farnley Junction. No.49327 had spent most of its life around the Birmingham area, being shedded at Aston prior to moving to Bescot. Both engines had paid their way and must have been accounted for as value for money by any count. Here they are shortly before the inevitable took place, just two of many of their kind which returned to their place of birth only to meet doom. *BLP - DB3120.*

Inside the scrap shed at Crewe Works on a Sunday in April 1964 with fallen 'Jubilee' No.45569 TASMANIA waiting for the Monday morning slaughter to begin. A long time resident of Holbeck shed, No.45569 was due to transfer to Patricroft but never made it and was instead cut up here before its withdrawal became official. That was the case with a lot of engines cut up at Crewe. They would come in for repair or overhaul, fail the inspection and get carted off to the scrapping shop before anybody realised. The withdrawal announcement usually post dating the demise. Behind the 'Jubilee' is Stanier Cl.4 tank No.42594, ex Carnforth, and another engine whose withdrawal post dated its actual cutting up. Two other tender engines can be seen in the dark recesses of the shop but what they were is unknown. *BLP DB6690.*

On the other side of the scrap shop that day was another 'Jubilee', No.45612 JAMAICA from Derby, along with ex Toton 4F No.44038 they probably travelled here together. Except for the big bits of former inmates, the shop floor is very clean and tidy. One can envisag the industry of this place Monday to Friday and Saturday mornings - incredible noise, lots of movement, smoke of varying thickness an odour, and an obvious sense of order. Now you see it, now you don't - well nearly. *BLP - DB6691.*